Neil & Diana
Kalinda

Lo

Tony

THE POETRY OF MR MINEVAR
Book 2

THE POETRY OF MR MINEVAR

BOOK 2

TONY RUSSELL

Copyright © 2023 Tony Russell

The moral right of the author has been asserted.

Apart from any fair dealing for the purposes of research or private study, or criticism or review, as permitted under the Copyright, Designs and Patents Act 1988, this publication may only be reproduced, stored or transmitted, in any form or by any means, with the prior permission in writing of the publishers, or in the case of reprographic reproduction in accordance with the terms of licences issued by the Copyright Licensing Agency. Enquiries concerning reproduction outside those terms should be sent to the publishers.

This is a work of fiction. Names, characters, businesses, places, events and incidents are either the products of the author's imagination or used in a fictitious manner. Any resemblance to actual persons, living or dead, or actual events is purely coincidental.

Troubador Publishing Ltd
Unit E2 Airfield Business Park
Harrison Road, Market Harborough
Leicestershire. LE16 7UL
Tel: 0116 279 2299
Email: books@troubador.co.uk
Web: www.troubador.co.uk/matador

ISBN 978 1 80313 748 3

British Library Cataloguing in Publication Data.
A catalogue record for this book is available from the British Library.

Printed and bound in Great Britain by 4edge Limited
Typeset in 11pt Minion Pro by Troubador Publishing Ltd, Leicester, UK

Matador is an imprint of Troubador Publishing Ltd

To my family
Mum, Dad*, Greg, Will & Imo
*1927–2018

We have to be deaf to the fools and listen to the wise.
　　　　　　　　　　　　　　　　　　　　　William Blake

You never know what is enough unless you know what is more than enough.
　　　　　　　　　　　　　　　　　　　　　William Blake

'One shot or two, Mr Minevar?'
'One is a very odd number, laddie. Two speaks of symmetry. Make it two and no spillage mind.'
　　　　　　　　　　　　　　　　　　　George Edward Minevar

CONTENTS

Prologue	xi
APHRODITE AND THE FRENCH CONNECTION	1
HENRY VIII	7
THE ALPHABET LIFE OF DR RICHARD ARBUTHNOT. THE BASTARD	12
THE TRIUMPH OF TOBY TORTOISE	17
PERFECTION	22
THE FLEA: FAME, SEDUCTION AND THE PLAGUE	24
GARDENER'S DELIGHT – MARRIAGE BLIGHT	31
MR MINEVAR GOES BESERK	37
SLEEP	40
THE WAR OF THE POESIES	48
THE CONFESSIONS OF TOBY WELLS	57
LITTLE OWL	66
EPILOGUE	72
MY HERO	72
THE POPE AND THE PECKERHEAD	74

PROLOGUE

I was the White Rabbit from *Alice in Wonderland* (*Oryctolagus cuniculus*). My appointment was for 2:00pm and my fob watch (I detest wrist watches) showed 2:28pm as I hurried along the country lane leading up to The George and Dragon. Stress, anxiety, and trepidation accompanied me on my short journey. I flew through the crowded saloon bar and hopped into the beer garden (hopped being le mot juste for beer and bunny). And there he was: Mr Minevar.

I had expected to see a face purple with rage. He is not a patient man. But no, he was stretched across the bench on his left side in a deep sleep. A faint smile had settled on his face – he was probably dreaming of carving the Sunday roast, for that was invariably his favourite dream. A breadcrumb was piggybacking a ride on a trickle of saliva meandering slowly down his left cheek. And I was shocked. Mr Minevar had ballooned in size to at least twenty stone.

As much as his weight gain, it was obvious that he had fallen on hard times; the jacket was shabby and the soles of his shoes were peppered with holes. His sweater likewise. Clearly this was a man in need of help. It was now way past our appointed time. To awake him or not, that was the question. I settled on giving the poet-of-sorts a further fifteen minutes and sat down to listen to his musical snoring. With the awakening, dear reader, we must add another animal – that is to say, a bear. I gave him a gentle knee-squeeze. Nothing. Then a bit harder and slowly, oh so slowly, he left the roast beef and Yorkshire pudding and awoke, much as a grizzly bear (*Ursus arctos horribilis*) exits its winter torpor. First there was limb stretching, then a blank stare, puzzlement and finally recognition. I heard the ursine grunt and then he grizzled, 'Oh, it's you. Why-oh-why did you wake me? I was about to carve…'

'I know, Mr Minevar, but we have an appointment. You said you would recite your poetry.'

'Indeed I did. I now remember.'

There was an awkward pause but I had to broach the subject.

'Mr Minevar, I hope you don't mind me mentioning this, but you seem to have gained weight and, excuse me for saying this, fallen on hard times.'

'Indeed I have. My poems are glued to the shelves and I have taken solace in comfort eating. In truth I have no future. I am flotsam and jetsam. Unwashed, unwanted, unhappy; a broken man.'

'Oh, Mr Minevar, you must not speak so ill of yourself. Your optimism had been usurped by self-pity I fear. No; keep buggering on, Mr Minevar, that was the mindset of Churchill: "KBO – never give up." Look, Mr Minevar, I have faith in you. You are my dear friend.' And I meant it. It was clear that his self-esteem needed a boost. A barrel load of TNT would raise it a little. Such were my thoughts.

'Mr Minevar, I mean George, I am extremely interested in what you say and write.'

Flattery, I know, but I thought it might help. Then I resorted to questioning him, much as a child would a parent.

'Who's your favourite poet, George? Or, failing that, what is your favourite quotation?'

Well, they say the eyes are connected to the soul, and within each eyeball there was a kind of glow. The pilot light had been lit.

'The answer to your first question laddie is Blake. As to the second question:

> "To see a world in a grain of sand
> And a heaven in a wildflower
> Hold infinity in the palm of your hand
> And eternity in an hour."

That's also a slice of Blake. Magical, it's all to do with imagination.'

Mr Minevar was entering first gear – gathering pace.

'You see, I think only Blake could have written those words. He had a hatred of so-called Reason, which was at the hub of the seventeenth- and eighteenth- century phenomenon known as the Enlightenment. Take a look at his painting of Newton, the quintessential creature of Reason – you won't find any warmth there. But, at the same time, and this is very interesting, he would not always jettison a contrary view; he believed "without contraries there is no progress". That is why he could write *The Marriage of Heaven and Hell*; an unlikely coupling I think you would agree.'

'Indeed I would, Mr Minevar, indeed I would. But any more Blakean quotes, George?'

'Oh, there are plenty, but I will give you just one. It is short but not sweet:

> "A robin redbreast in a cage
> Puts all heaven in a rage."

You see, Blake could not abide cruelty towards man or beast. Now *tempus fugit*; we must move on.'

And that urgency pleased me. Just entering his second gear, I thought.

'Well, George, what can you offer your hungry student today?'

'It is an eclectic mix. In no particular order: Aphrodite, Henry VIII, gardening, sleep. Then there is one of my early poems concerning that creature from the swamp, Dr Arbuthnot.'

Mr Minevar's face became a traffic light, red with anger, then a jaundiced yellow before vomit-green. The mere mention of Arbuthnot's name often elicited such a response. It's called "The Alphabet Life of Dr Richard Arbuthnot. The Bastard." There is also a poem concerning a tortoise and a hare.'

'A smorgasbord of poems, Mr Minevar.'

'Perhaps. There is also a poem with more than a nod to science; it is called "Perfection". Then there is "The Flea" (not the full title, laddie), and "The Confessions of Toby Wells". Finally, "Little Owl ". That's my favourite,' added Mr Minevar.

'Well, "eclectic" certainly fits the bill. Where to start, George?'

'Aphrodite, of course, you young turnip-head.'

Now Mr Minevar has a number of faults; often minor,

but there are one or two that can irritate quite a lot, in particular his pomposity and condescension. He treats me as a numbskull, and although I'm not the sharpest knife in the drawer, his attitude does not do him any favours. You'll notice these traits I'm sure as you read on.

'I'm afraid I know very little about Aphrodite, George.'

'I thought so. Well sit back and learn. The Greeks had a penchant for relating unusual births. Athena for instance exited from Zeus's forehead fully clothed and fully armed; no midwife in sight.'

'Gosh, how odd!'

'No interruptions. Aphrodite's birth was equally bizarre. The titan Cronos castrated his dad Ouranos and chucked his genitals into the sea. One can imagine the high pitch of the scrotal cry. Anyway, our beloved Aphrodite was born from the resultant foam caused by the splash of his genitals.'

Involuntarily I crossed my legs. I desperately wanted to ask questions but heeded his request for silence.

'So out of pain was born Beauty,' said Mr Minevar.

'A lot of mothers would agree to that, George.'

'Quite so. Now the point is these gods and goddesses enjoyed toying with us mortals, and it is highly probable that beneath Aphrodite's stunning looks there may have been a degree of naughtiness; that is the subject matter of my poem in which she causes a poor chap to lose his mother tongue, English, to be replaced by French. He could speak French but not understand the lingo when it was spoken to him. Odd, not logical, but it is what it is, as they say.'

Mr Minevar looked at me and could see I was itching to ask a question.

'No questions; just listen!'

APHRODITE AND THE FRENCH CONNECTION

'Aphrodite pulls the strings
And mischief to our love-life brings
Causing much erectile dysfunction
She does this with the least compunction.

And ladies are not left scot-free
As she can infect them with V.D.
Chlamydial pain though quite severe
Is nothing compared to gonorrhoea.

She's vain, capricious, and a tease,
Who specialises in herpes,
And when two lovers meet and kiss,
She curses them with syphilis.

She plays around with our libido
And giggles when it hits an all-time low.
Frustrated lovers are bewildered;
Puzzled why the foreplay's slow'

'Oh, the little pixie!' I exclaimed. But Mr Minevar had reached third gear and ignored me.

> 'But sometimes she plays a peculiar game
> When you both lie knackered on the bed.
> Her target is the English male;
> She infiltrates his English head.
>
> Ensuring no English can be spoken
> 'Tis only French that can be heard
> From his lips, this foreign language;
> It's so bizarre, odd and absurd.

Mr Minevar interrupted himself:
'Have you got a girlfriend, laddie? I myself am wedded to the monastic life.'

'You speak oxymoronically, Mr Minevar, but no, only a cat called Bartholomew. My friends call him Bartholo<u>meow</u>, which is a bit childish.'

'Yes, puerile; I dislike intensely anything puerile.'

'Same here, Mr Minevar; anyway, back to Bartholomew. He's very fluffy. A tabby. A fluffy tabby. A little overweight. A flabby, fluffy tabby. A flabby, fluffy, tubby tabby.'

'Yes, yes, I understand.' And, wishing he had not asked me the question, he continued. And curiously it seemed to be autobiographical.

> 'Now, as it happens my girlfriend's bilingual,
> Born in France: raised in Versailles.
> Five years ago she crossed the channel
> And made her home in cosy Rye.

> Ah! the first occasion comes back to me
> She had given me this adoring look.
> "Darling, it's time for pillow talk
> Turn off the telly, put down your book."
>
> A little miffed, for I do love reading—'

'Woah, woah, stop, Mr Minevar! Oh my! Oh dear! Oh heavens! That's a wee bit selfish. It would appear that reading takes precedence over this lady. Oh my! Oh dear! Oh heavens!'

I had spoken too much, I know this because Mr Minevar glared at me, said nothing and continued afresh:

> 'A little miffed for I do love reading
> Especially poems by Keats or Shelley
> So *Ozymandias* had to wait
> I put down my book, switched off the telly.
>
> <u>*And then it happened:*</u>
> "Ma chère Marie vraiment je t'adore"
> I think translated means "I love you"
> The language of love so impressed her
> She replied, "George, tu es un peu fou!"
>
> Not understanding what she had said
> I gave a kind of Gallic shrug.
> "Pourquoi le shrug?" she said in Franglais
> I answered with an English hug.'

I felt the urge to speak.

'Do you think Aphrodite made a habit of doing this, Mr Minevar?'

'A good question, for it is now that the poem, albeit briefly, takes on an historical perspective – to Georgian England; in fact to the days of "Rule Britannia", Nelson and Lady Hamilton.'

Mr Minevar cleared his throat, sucked in several litres of air and continued:

> 'Turning John Bull into Gallic Cockerel
> Aphrodite enjoys her tricksy play.
> Nelson aborted lusty Emma's advances,
> By saying he was "trop fatigué"

'Oh, cruel Aphrodite!' I ejaculated. 'And there is indeed a French connection to Lady H.'

"Indeed so. She died in Calais impoverished, neglected and unloved by England. But to continue:

> But my Marie likes our tête-a-têtes
> French or English, it does not matter
> Though I'm sure she thinks her cher George
> "Vraiment es fou" – mad as a hatter!
>
> So there you have it: The French connection.
> An oddity it must be said.
> When bleu, blanc, rouge; the Tricolore
> Usurps our flag of white and red.
>
> And when Aphrodite has had her fun
> Turning her god-gaze to other stuff

The linguistic twist now boring her
She switches off; she's had enough.'

'Well, Mr Minevar, she is certainly powerful'
'Oui, c'est vrai… elle est très puissante.'
I looked startled.
'Laddie, I'm only joking.'
And I'm glad to say a smile played upon his lips.
'Dear boy, I can see the barman playing a tune with his fingers and thumbs. I would that he were not idle.'
'I see – a drink then, Mr Minevar? Lager or beer?'
'Oh no no,No!',Mr Minevar crescendoed,' I have entered the spirit world. In particular, cocktails. I believe there is one called <u>French Connection</u>.'
'To say is to do.' And two minutes later I returned to the table and, in a mangled French accent and with a flourish, said:
'Voilà, monsieur,votre cocktail.'
'I thank thee – tu es très gentil.'

N.B. All the cocktails in the book are *bona fide*.

1 Henry VIII (1491–1547)

HENRY VIII

'Well, that barman got the mixture just right, Mr Minevar.'

'Yes, he's a credit to The George and Dragon. His name is Alfredo Borelli Silviano del Potro. I call him Alf.'

'Alf the shaker, the cocktail maker, eh, Mr Minevar?'

'Quite so. Now my next poem is about a monster of a man: Henry VIII.'

And without further ado, he was off:

'If you want to learn about Henry VIII:

> Take great pains to avoid malarkey
> By tuning into David Starkey.
> Succinct, enlightening, without a doubt
> He knows our Henry inside out.

That will please Dr Starkey,' said Mr Minevar, looking chuffed. 'Anyway,' added Mr Minevar, 'here's *my* take on Henry:

> King Henry was a tyrant king
> The cause of so much suffering.
> Married to Cath of Aragon
> It was Anne Boleyn who turned him on.

> So desperate was he to sire an heir
> When Anne bore a girl, he was in despair.
> Renouncing what was the marriage bed,
> On false pretences chopped off her head—'

'With a sword.' I interrupted. 'Less messy.'
'Same result,' said Mr Minevar and continued:

> 'Then his roving eye saw Jane Seymour
> And to his joy a boy she bore.
> But alas poor Jane quite quickly died
> So that roving eye roamed far and wide.
>
> When Holbein's *Anne of Cleves* was seen,
> It appeared that Henry was quite keen.
> But seen in the flesh, he was aghast
> And knew the marriage would not last.'

'Apparently she was too busty, Mr Minevar. Top heavy. Anne of Cleavage, you might say, Mr Minevar.'
'Indeed so, you interrupting bluebottle. Please allow me to continue:

> So on to Cath Howard, wife number five
> Who was so vivacious, so alive,
> But in the past she'd slept around
> So without her head she went into the ground.
>
> Wife number six was Cathy Parr
> Who had the most common sense by far.
> Respectful, loving, she cared for him
> And in 1547 she buried him.'

Here Mr Minevar interrupted himself and said that 1547 should be read as individual numbers.

'It helps with the rhythm,' he said, almost apologetically. I thought he had finished but no, he cleared his throat with a swig of <u>French Connection</u> and continued:

> 'But who was this man we think we know
> Who thin to fat did quickly grow?
> When young a kind of Renaissance lad;
> When old was gouty, grumpy, sad.
>
> When young he jousted and played the lute
> Well versed in literature was he
> But all this changed with passing years;
> He lost his love for poetry.'

'Well, Mr Minevar, he certainly had several strings to his bow.' But Mr Minevar ignored me.

> 'Yes, Henry was a tyrant king
> Who split from Rome to marry Anne.
> He bled the monasteries dry;
> He was the Reformation man.'

'I think Thomas Cromwell could also take credit for that, Mr Minevar, as I believe he oversaw the demise of about eight hundred monasteries.'

'Indeed, that is so. But to continue:

> Alas Henry killed so many folks
> Citing both heresy and treason.

> Folks disliked how he usurped the Church
> As paranoia robbed him of reason—'

'Some historians reckon he may have killed more than 50,000 people,' I interjected. But again, there was no recognition of my existence.

> 'Ask any person on the street
> What legacy from him survives,
> They shrug and say, "I'm not sure
> But I know for certain he had six wives!"
>
> Yes, Henry was a tyrant king
> Who took from the church when he was needy
> But *six* wives, Henry, that's excessive
> For Christ's sake, Henry, it's downright greedy.'

I waited for more words, but no words were spoken except for these:

'There is no humidity in this wretched climate of ours; curse global warming.'

'Meaning what Mr Minevar?'

'Dry; I'm almost mummified'

'You are cursed with thirst Mr M.So, what's it to be ?'

'I rather fancy another cocktail, something very refreshing, something from the East – a <u>Singapore Sling</u>.'*

And you could have spun me around a dozen times, blindfolded me for good measure and I would have still

---

* Gin, cherry brandy, Bénédictine, angostura bitters, pineapple juice, lime juice, ice.

found my way to the bar. On returning, I spoke to him as you might to a child. It was both catharsis and a manifestation of my annoyance with his parsimony.

'And what do you say?'

'Thank thee, I thank thee.'

And unlike Henry, who had gone thin to fat, I could see that my wallet would rapidly be going from fat to thin.

THE ALPHABET LIFE OF DR RICHARD ARBUTHNOT. THE BASTARD

'I must say, Mr Minevar, that Alf is a wizard when it comes to making cocktails.'

'Indeed, he is.'

'Shame that Henry VIII and his cronies missed out.'

Whilst I was thinking of names for Henry's cocktails – something like <u>Head On The Block</u>, or a <u>Bloody Henry</u> which would have foreshadowed the famous <u>Bloody Mary</u> – Mr Minevar was lost in thought.

'I think the best cocktail name would be <u>Hanged Drawn and Quartered</u>, Mr Minevar; a gruesome name but Alf would probably concoct a very fine, delicious cocktail, don't you agree?'

But I was not on Mr Minevar's radar. I soon found out why.

'You are aware of my arch foe, that odious creature Dr Arbuthnot?'

'Indeed, I am, Mr Minevar.'

'Well, my first poem concerning this parasitic worm

was written twenty years ago. It is plainly a poem of little consequence save that I was correct to take an immediate dislike to the man, regarding him a malevolent beast who abused hospitality and took great delight in spreading malicious gossip, in the process destroying many an innocent person. And my judgement was thus: vile, obnoxious, toxic. I had read a couple of his spiteful reviews before observing his disgusting behaviour at a party. No words can fully describe the toad, but I cemented into his life, by means of a poem, a few letters of the alphabet.'

'Well, I'm all ears, Mr Minevar.'

Mr Minevar cleared his throat and began the recital:

> 'Dr Arbuthnot whom I've just met
> Reminds me of the alphabet.
> So impolite and short of fuse
> He always forgets his P's and Q's.
>
> To any party he attends
> Disruption follows in his wake.
> The host too late realises
> The invitation's a huge mistake.
>
> The parasite would drink till drunk
> Abusing hospitality.
> The greedy sod is thus refuelled
> By excess booze and cups of T.'

'I believe you have mentioned to me that he also stuffs his fat face with food; pies, nuts, crisps, sandwiches, cake; nothing goes untouched, am I right, Mr Minevar?'

'Indeed, you are.'

> 'With belly full as well as bladder
> His satyr-mind says, "It's time to flee."
> And pointing Percy to the rose bush
> He baptises it with his P.
>
> Then homeward bound the bounder heads
> Still sozzled, he drives erratically,
> Arriving at his penthouse suite
> That overlooks the Irish C.
>
> So, Arbuthnot, such is your life
> So hedonistic it's but a farce
> An empty life, lived by a fool
> Who knows not his elbow from his R's.
>
> So, there you have him: Arbuthnot
> Within this poem 'tis plain to see
> Pilfered from the alphabet;
> P, Q and T, R and C.'

'Not weighty I know,' said Mr Minevar. 'No matter, after all it was written two decades ago when I was, as Dylan Thomas would have it, "young and easy under the apple boughs." Yes, and "happy as the grass was green."'

'Absolutely, Mr Minevar. I wonder if I could have a try, Mr M?'

'Of course.' Then he added rather ungraciously, 'If you must.'

I cleared my throat with a sip of Singapore Sling. And this was my sling-shot.

'Arbuthnot, you just take the biscuit
Not one word you say is ever true
The lies pour out by pen on paper
Truth is a word not known to U.

Self-deluded this selfish oaf
Believes he's the king of repartee.
No wit or wisdom; only words that sting
That are much more waspish than a B.

So, there you have him: Arbuthnot
Within this poem that is brand new,
Two letters from the alphabet
Clearly seen: both B and U.'

'You latched on quite quickly.'

'Thank you, Mr Minevar.'

'Now, I think we have had quite enough of the alphabet and that slimeball.'

But Mr Minevar had unleashed me. I was a free man. I continued:

'So it's back to basics for Arbuthnot
He must first learn the alphabet
Then nouns and verbs and adjectives
But what goes where he'll soon forget.

And what he writes is so appalling,
It beggars belief that he is read.
Each page I liken to toilet paper
To flush down the loo or else to shred.'

'All right. You've had your fun. Enough of Arbuthnot.'

But no, I was determined to continue with the Arbuthnot Assassination. And I did.

> 'There's a huge chip upon his shoulder
> Perhaps that's why he attacks with verve,
> Looking for chinks within your armour,
> Hoping to hit that vital nerve.
>
> He reminds me of a great dung beetle
> Who rolls out shit every day.
> But the beetle-dung serves a purpose
> Unlike his work which has naught to say.'

'Stop! No more! I beg, desist; put the Bastard and Mrs Alphabet to bed.'

'I'm sorry, Mr Minevar, I got carried away.'

'Apology accepted. I know the feeling; sometimes you have an itch that has to be scratched or a thirst that has to be quenched. Yes, a thirst.'

'Do you fancy another cocktail, Mr Minevar?'

'Indeed, I do. And rather fortuitously there is a new cocktail called XYZ.[†] Alf will have heard of it.'

And sure enough he had.

[†] Rum, orange liqueur, lemon juice.

THE TRIUMPH OF TOBY TORTOISE

Well, there we were, two men sipping our cocktails. Both of us feeling relaxed and contented; in clover you might say. And that put me in mind of tortoises, as I know they eat both leaf and flower of this beautiful little plant. It was my turn to start the conversation.

'Do you like tortoises, Mr Minevar?'

'An odd question, right out of the blue. Yes, I do. Why do you ask?'

'Oh, I just wondered.'

'I don't suppose you've read *Aesop's Fables*?'

There was, as usual, more than a whiff of condescension.

'As a matter of fact, Mr Minevar, I have. *The Ant and the Grasshopper*, *The Frog and the Fox* and of course *The Tortoise and the Hare*. I could go on.'

'Please don't,' said Mr Minevar.

There was a pause while I licked my wounds. Then something miraculous happened: Mr Minevar apologised.

'Sorry, I was a wee bit harsh, stopping you in mid-flow like that.'

'Quite all right, Mr Minevar. No problem.'

Another pause as I gave my wound a final lick. It was my turn to break the silence.

'I love nature, Mr Minevar, both fauna and flora. It gives me goose bumps.'

The avian allusion was unintended.

'Quite so. But back to Aesop. In particular his fable, *The Tortoise and the Hare*. I wrote a poem concerning these two animals and I borrowed quite freely from that fable. Not plagiarism mind; I just borrowed the gist of the story.'

And this is what I heard:

> 'They were under starter's orders
> But the race did not seem fair
> As the competitors were so very different:
> Toby Tortoise and Henry Hare.
>
> The shot rang out; the race had started
> And the hare sped off with speed.
> Only several seconds had elapsed
> But so enormous was his lead.
>
> Only then did Toby begin to move a leg
> And with slow deliberation another.
> (Meanwhile Henry Hare was having lunch
> With his mum and younger brother.)
>
> His mother said, "Dear, have *one* drink
> I know you've got the time,
> There's brandy, whisky, gin and tonic
> Or dandelion wine."

'Mr Minevar, it's a bit irresponsible for a parent to offer a mere child alcohol.'

' Indeed so ,but other animals indulge. You have no doubt heard the saying "drunk as a skunk."'

'Yes, I have. Oh, wait a minute: pissed as a newt! That's quite a common expression.'

'Quite so.'

'Also, I have been rat-arsed a few times, Mr Minevar.'

'I'm sure you have. Now, my little dipsomaniac, I shall continue:

> So back to Toby: he was on the move,
> Less than 0.1 mile an hour.
> Though his heart rate was 150:
> He was running at full power.
>
> But Henry Hare was still drinking.
> Mum viewed him with concern..
> He was always rather cocky
> Would the poor child never learn?
>
> "Dear, I would suggest you *go*"
> "No, Mum, this race is in my pocket,
> As with alcohol within my veins
> I'm faster than a rocket."
>
> And so he stayed and over-quenched his thirst
> And then he had a snooze.
> Yes, the silly hare-brain had drunk too much,
> So full was he with booze.

And Toby, well he just plodded on
And overtook the hare.
The finish line within his sight
Just one hour and he'd be there.

And, of course, you know the ending
The tortoise won the race
Focused and determined
His speed a steady pace.'

'And what did that mean to Toby Mr Minevar?'
'It gave him a sense of achievement. Yes, if he could have smiled, he would have done so. But I'll continue:

Well, this is a preachy poem
The kind you've read elsewhere,
Where the temperance of the tortoise
Contrasts with the hedonistic hare

Who was much too over-confident
And would not heed advice.
Booze clouded Henry's judgement
And thus he paid the price.'

'And the moral, Mr Minevar?'
'This would be my take:

'Be patient and be focused
Never waver from your goal
Yes, keep to the path you've chosen
And you'll find contentment in your soul.'

'Aye aye to that, Mr Minevar. A drink, Mr Minevar? In a Toby jug, perhaps?'

And with a smile he said. 'No thanks. I'll give temperance a try. Just this once mind'

PERFECTION

'Do you believe in perfection, Mr Minevar?'

'Indeed, I do and, please, call me George.'

'Yes of course, George it is. What would be your choice of something that deserves such an accolade?'

'I believe it was the great writer and aviator Antoine de Saint-Exupéry who said, "Perfection is achieved, not where there is nothing more to add, but when there is nothing left to take away." I believe you need look no further than Einstein's equation $E = mc^2$.'

'Yes, it is such a beautiful equation, George.'

'Actually, I scribbled a few lines about that equation.'

And like a magician a piece of crumpled paper appeared in his hand.

'Written long ago when I had more energy and less mass.'

And this is what I heard:

'There is no equation that can be compared
To Einstein's $E = mc^2$
Relating mass and energy
'Tis a law of such simplicity,
Yet so profound; a Universal law

> A gem, a diamond with no flaw.
> Unlocking Nature's mysterious ways,
> Einstein deserves our utmost praise.
> His genius with the world he shared
> The immortal, $E = mc^2$.'

'Yes,' continued Mr Minevar, 'as I say in the poem, he unearthed a Universal Law. And it is so simple. As Alexander Pope wrote, "There is majesty in simplicity."'

'Aye, aye to that, George. It's perfect. But although it relates to light, it would also be true to say there is a dark side to the equation as it explains the power unleashed by the atomic bomb.'

'Quite so; it is up to Mankind to use this hidden energy wisely. It could be the salvation of Mankind or sound an extremely loud death knell.'

I thought the conversation was getting a little too morbid for my liking.

'Well, Einstein played around with time and I think it's time for some refreshments. So, what's your tipple, George?'

'I rather fancy an Einstein Martini.'[‡]

'So do I.'

And so it was that the two cocktails were ordered, and I was back at the table in no time at all. Relativitally speaking!

[‡] Dry gin, dry vermouth, Spanish olives, lemon peel.

THE FLEA: FAME, SEDUCTION AND THE PLAGUE

'Einstein was a genius was he not, George?'
'Indeed, he was.'
'Nifty with the violin as well as top of the scientific tree.'
'Just so.'
'Newton was very clever wasn't he, George?'
'Yes.'

Well, as you can see, Mr Minevar wasn't in a talkative mood. Silence ensued. Then I thought I would jump start a conversation away from those two colossi.

'George, you're an animal lover. What floats your boat? For me, it's the elephant, gorilla or any one of the cetaceans – probably the dolphin. Yes, I think the dolphin would be my choice.'

No reply forthcoming, I repeated the question.

'For me there is only one creature that ticks all the boxes and that of course is the flea.'

'Are you pulling my leg, George?'

'No, no, the flea gets the gold medal every time. A survivor;

a miracle of nature. You can't cuddle it or take it for walks but, my God, you can learn about it and marvel at its athleticism – and reflect on how things might have been different.'

'I was following you until the endpoint, then I lost my compass.'

Mr Minevar was getting animated; on fire one might say. I feel he would have been a firm friend of that wonderful lady Miriam Rothschild who was a great flea expert. Well, as is often the case with Mr Minevar, he proceeded to give me a short history lesson before reciting his poem. It was time to tune into Radio Minevar.

'Have you heard of the bubonic plague ?'

'Indeed, I have, Mr Minevar.'

'And do you realise the full extent of the impact it had on Mankind?'

'Not really.'

'I thought as much. Well, lend me your ears. In 500 BC, Athens succumbed to the plague; a major casualty was Pericles the great orator. Fast forward to 6AD and there was the so-called Justinian plague, but most folks are familiar with the plague of the fourteenth century which swept East to West, ravaging Europe: The Black Death; a sobriquet, I believe, given in Victorian times. With me so far?'

'Yes, Mr Minevar.'

'Now the causative agent was unknown – many thought it was the act of God; angry because of the wicked ways of Man. Indeed, you had flagellants whipping themselves as punishment. But it was not the wrath of God: it was the potent, toxic combination of flea and rat. The Black Rat (*Rattus rattus*). Although some historians have questioned whether Mr Flea was totally to blame, that is to say lice have been implicated. But what *is* certain is that the disease was bacterial: *Yersinnia pestis*.'

'Ok, but I still don't understand your admiration for this wretched insect that caused so much suffering.'

'A fair point but can you not marvel at its form and function? Built like a miniature tank, can leap enormous distances, and has an extremely rapid reproduction rate. When Man has blown himself up, what will be left: cockroaches, Eliot's crabs scuttling across the sea floor, and the flea.'

'And tardigrades, Mr Minevar. But you may well be right. Bartholomew had fleas once and it was a devil to get rid of them.'

"Indeed so. A bit more history; the plague kept recurring. About twenty-five million people died in the fourteenth century, a terrible statistic. Jobs were plentiful and wages rose as the workers could demand higher wages. Economic consequences, dear boy. In the Great Plague of London (1664–66) about 100,000 died. It is still around today, but antibiotics can be given, and deaths are very few.'

'I see what you mean about its role in human history, but I would still have my dolphin any day.'

'Well, there is no poem about your dolphin; Mr Flea is centre stage. Here are my scribbles:

> I am an arthropodic acrobat
> With leaps defying gravity.
> "*Xenopsylla cheopis*" is my name,
> But you can call me simply flea.
>
> So well-drawn by Robert Hooke,
> His *Micrographia* was well known.

Having viewed me through his microscope,
He made me the toast of London town.

Folks marvelled at my scaly skin,
My hairy legs, so many jointed.
Astonished by my segmented coat,
And mouthparts, sharp, so very pointed.

With ease they pierce the human skin;
Syringe and needle all in one.
I'm even the subject of seduction;
Just read the poem by John Donne.'

'Stop, Mr Minevar! I'm so sorry to interrupt, but I do not know of this man John Donne.'

'Poetical interruptus! Mid-poem you wish me to give you another potted history?'

'Yes, please .'

'Very well. I shall deal with the mid-rendition interruption and then continue.

'Donne was an English poet of the seventeenth century whose work was highly intellectual. He was a master of conceit, whereby one pairs off dissimilar subjects but then, and here is the nub, he very cleverly conjures up a connection between these apparently unrelated entities. Are you with me?'

'Yes, Mr Minevar. So far.'

'Well, Donne was the chief member of like-minded poets: The Metaphysical Poets. Do you want me to expand?'

'Yes please, Mr Minevar.'

'Well, he was also a writer of beautiful love poems, epigrams and satires. In addition, he penned sermons: he became Dean of St Paul's, laddie. I could go on, but time is short. You may recall, before the interruption, I was about to touch on the flea and seduction. Please note the poetic voice of the flea. You see the mingling of the blood from man and mistress is likened to sex. And the addition of the flea makes a Trinity. That is to say, there is more than a whiff of religiosity. It's all in the poem.'

And so, Mr Minevar hit the restart button.

'Here the speaker tries seduction
Using a metaphor – a flea.
As I have bitten both him and mistress
A Trinity exists of them and me.

Mixed blood within me thus unified
They, just like sex, have become one.
Its clever, witty, even religious
So all can say "Well done, John Donne".

But back to matters much more serious
A world away from poetry
We enter into the world of numbers
Depopulation caused by me.

Little did the poor folk know
By rat- travel I moved with ease
And sowed the seeds of devastation
The carrier of a vile disease.

So pernicious was depopulation
From East to West throughout the land.

> One secret bite was all it took;
> In mass slaughter, I *was* the hand.
>
> From feeding did the microbe <u>Yersinia</u>
> Enter the blood of rich and poor,
> The unseen cause of panic, suffering
> A much one-sided kind of war.
>
> Fever, headache, fatigue, delirium
> Swollen lymph nodes, shallow breath
> Told you your body's fight was failing
> Your destination: a painful death.
>
> Sending so many to their grave
> I changed the course of History;
> So small my body, so great the loss
> By me the humble jumping flea.'

'Well, Mr Minevar, you were true to the title; fame, seduction and the plague. Perhaps my dolphin has competition after all.'

But Mr Minevar wasn't paying attention; he was looking at his empty glass.

'The contents of my tumbler seem to have evaporated; absolutely bone dry.'

'Same again, Mr M?'

'No, I rather fancy a cocktail called <u>Lion's Tail</u>.§ I thank thee.'

Then he added a note of caution.

---

§   Bourbon, pimento dram, citrus bitters, and simple syrup.

'And no spillage on the return journey.'

A wee bit cheeky I thought.

'No worries, Mr M. My hand is as steady as the Rock of Gibraltar.'

And two minutes later he was sipping from a full glass of Lion's Tail; i.e. no history of a spillage.

GARDENER'S DELIGHT- MARRIAGE BLIGHT

'Crikey, Mr Minevar, I think this <u>Lion's Tail</u> has gone to my head; I feel quite squiffy. To coin a phrase, heads and tails, that's what I am, Mr Minevar.'

'Take some slow deep breaths; too much bourbon for my liking. I must have a word with Alf.'

I filled my lungs just as he suggested and soon felt better. The air was pure and I could detect the scent of honeysuckle. And that set me off.

'Do you like gardening, Mr Minevar?'

'It is my umbilical cord to Gaia, Mother Earth, and it is one of the most creative hobbies one can have. Francis Bacon, the natural philosopher, said it was "the purest of human pleasures."'

'Yes, I agree with Francis.'

'Many wise people have extolled the virtues of gardening. You've heard of Voltaire, no doubt?'

'Indeed, I have, Mr Minevar.'

'"*Il faut cultiver notre jardin*", that's what he said – we must cultivate our garden.'

'From his famous book *Candide*.'

'Quite so. It's a metaphor, of course: we've all been allotted a patch of time, as it were, and we've got to make the most of it. Time is short: ask your ancestors. But Voltaire was handy with the hoe, deft with the dibber, as well as being gifted with the quill.'

Mr Minevar took a sip of his cocktail and winced a little as it burnt a trail to his stomach. Yes, Alf, you overdid the bourbon. Mr Minevar burped then continued.

'Gardening is both a science and an art. Take Monet for instance, the great Impressionist painter. He created the most beautiful garden at Giverny.'

'Have you been there, Mr Minevar?'

'Indeed, I have. He was very proud of his garden: "My garden is my most beautiful masterpiece", such were his thoughts.'

He took another sip of cocktail then began to speak again.

'Now, I do not claim to be a Monet—'

'Of course not.'

'Few can, but I *can* claim to know a thing or two about the fruits of my labour.'

'I'm sure you can, Mr Minevar. You know everything.'

There was an awkward silence, before he continued:

'My speciality,' said Mr Minevar, 'is growing tomatoes, my favourite being <u>Gardener's Delight</u> (*Lycopersicon esculentum*). Small fruit, tall plant, which you must stake well in moist and fertile soil. Anyway, the point is that I wrote a poem having wedded tomatoes and marriage and it does *not* relate to them being so-called love-apples. In fact, quite the opposite; it concerns the *perils* of gardening.'

'I should not have thought gardening particularly perilous, Mr Minevar.'

'Perhaps not. But listen to the lady in my poem.' And this is what I heard:

> 'We got married in the month of May
> In that splendid city that's called York.
> That photo shows me with the Maid of Honour
> And *that* photo shows him with his garden fork.
>
> He's most at home with garden tools
> And loves to wield his secateurs.
> He uses them so judiciously,
> He earns the envy of his peers.
>
> But I digress – back to the marriage
> A huge mistake I'm afraid.
> While I lay frustrated on my bed
> He was double-digging with his spade.

'I think I can see where this is going, Mr Minevar.'
'No doubt you can, you interrupting nematode.'
I think the indigestion had made him a bit grumpy. Anyway:

> 'When autumn came, denuding trees
> I cried, "Come inside, for heaven's sake
> I am your wife in need of love."
> But the deaf-eared lummox had lost his rake—'

'Oh, the poor woman; the man is obsessed. He's lost his marbles as well as his rake, Mr Minevar.'
'Yes, quite. Any more interruptions and I shall stop. I am working my way through the poem in seasonal fashion.

When winter-cold knocked at our door
Oh, how wet winds did blow and howl.
In pouring rain, the stupid man
Was toiling with his trusty—'

'Trowel,' I whispered.

'Then spring arrived with better weather
So very quickly did plant life grow
I stayed inside to do spring cleaning
While the numbskull weeded with his—'

'Hoe,' said I, sotto voce.

'Again came summer, with all its glory
The best there had been for many years.
And one could view from the lounge window
Topiary fashioned by his shears.'

Personally, I was finding this poem pedestrian, but I nodded along, encouraging Mr Minevar who was suffering from 'bourbonitis'. Anyway, dear reader, we are nearly at the end.

'But of all the plants that he cared for
And ladled love both day and night
'Tis strange but true, it was a tomato
Whose happy name is <u>Gardener's Delight</u>.'

Nearly there. Not far to go.

> 'But my stance on this is so very different
> Concerning that name: 'Gardener's Delight'.
> It fills me with hate and utmost loathing
> 'Tis a major cause of my marriage blight.'

Just one more verse, dear reader.

> 'As I am under no illusion
> A country girl like me has wed
> A man who is married to his garden
> And left me chaste, alone in bed.'

There, the eagle has landed. Words that were spoken when a man finally landed on the moon and exactly my thoughts when this bloody poem had ended.

'Now that story is very very sad, Mr Minevar. One wonders whether there are many "gardening widows". My feeling is that the allotment and golf course seem to act like magnets to the male sex. But on a more cheerful note, Mr Minevar, whatever the season, you're up for a cocktail. So, what's it to be?'

'A Red Snapper;⁋ both a fish (*Lutjanus campechanus*) and a cocktail. It's Alf's specialty, so I've been told. Never had it myself.'

I didn't think the Snapper would do much for his indigestion. And when I returned with two large cocktails, Mr Minevar had turned slightly pink, very much like the colour of this much underrated fish.

Oh, I've got a brain like a sieve! I nearly forgot to mention

---

⁋ Gin, tomato juice, lemon juice, Tabasco, Worcester sauce, celery, salt and black pepper.

that the next section doesn't deal with Mr Minevar's poetry; rather it concerns Mr Minevar himself. And it has a title: <u>Mr Minevar Goes Beserk</u>.

MR MINEVAR GOES BESERK

What I am about to write describes an extraordinary and unsettling event. It pains me even to have a fleeting thought about it, so I shall be as brief as possible.

You will recall that Mr Minevar and I were in the beer garden of the George and Dragon. When I arrived, it was warm outside and extremely relaxing to sip our cocktails and chat. Mr Minevar has no time for small talk, but I think this is a mistake. After all, from acorns do oak trees grow. Anyway, quite suddenly, a wild gust of wind blew across the beer garden and I thought it might be wise to enter inside. I said as much. Mr Minevar looked at me, aghast.

'Well, Mr Minevar, there is a large cumulonimbus cloud heading our way. I think it prudent to—'

'Would Robert Falcon Scott have slunk into the bar defeated by a mere cloud? Would he? No, no, he would not.'

Mr Minevar's speech accelerated markedly; almost auctioneer's speed.

'Would Ranulph Twisleton-Wykeham Fiennes have picked up his skis and tampons—'

'Crampons,' Mr Minevar.'

'Suckrack—'

'Rucksack, Mr Minevar.'

'And gone home to his slippers and hot chocolate? No, he would not. My God, Ranulph Twisleton-Wykeham Fiennes, what a tornado of a name. Lord how it does exercise my tongue. How the name does spiral out of my mouth: me buccal cavity is a veritable vortex; a mouth of maelstroms. All praise to his parents for giving him such a turbulence of names. What was it Lear said in defiance of the storm?'

And here Mr Minevar stood up, shook his fist at the sky and hoovered in ten litres of air before bellowing:

'"Blow, winds and crack your cheeks! Rage! Blow! You cataracts and hurricanoes spout. Till you have drenched our steeples – drowned the cocks!" No, we stay. I shall not succumb to mere vapour; of sterner stuff are we made. We stay, rooted and ready.'

And he stood like an oak tree: tall, proud, erect, and determined to withstand the 'storm'.

Well of course, dear reader, one can't blame global warming for this meteorological madness; the only storm was the one raging in his head. An overheated brain; too many neurons firing all at once leading to cranial chaos. I was at a loss. Then I appealed to his love of cocktails.

He shouted his reply as if he was in a gale force wind. A bit like that fine actor Brian Blessed; stentorian. 'Why, there is only one cocktail for this perilous predicament: 'tis a <u>Hurricane Cocktail</u>."'

** Light rum, dark rum, passion fruit, orange juice, half a lime and grenadine syrup. Orange slices and maraschino cherries for garnish. With or without ice.

'Well, I'll just nip off and fetch a couple.'

Heaven only knows what goes on in his brainbox. There was no gale, just a breeze.

'Aye, laddie, I thank thee. Leave me to fight the elements. I shall not fail.'

So off I went. Luckily the cumulonimbus monster missed us, and when I returned the sun had lit up the beer garden. Warmth and hopefully sanity had returned as an exhausted Mr Minevar had sloughed off Lear and morphed into Rip Van Winkle, being sound asleep. And, dear reader, it is sleep that will be our next port of call.

SLEEP

'Mr Minevar, do you mind if I ask you a question?'

'Possibly not.'

'Well, when I arrived for our appointment, you were sound asleep and—'

'Was I smiling?'

'Well, yes, actually you were, Mr Minevar and dribbling.'

'If I was smiling, I was in the warm embrace of Morpheus, bringer of dreams.'

He ignored my reference to dribbling.

'I see.'

Mr Minevar's face grew stern and his voice stuffed to the gills with emotion. 'But beware of his brother Epiales; he fills your soul with terror. You awake in a cold sweat, heart racing, confused, perhaps terrified. Some unspeakable terror has caused a tsunami of hormones, adrenaline and cortisol to name but two. Moreover, laddie.' —

'I'm sorry to interrupt, Mr Minevar, but I was going to say that after your "funny turn", when you railed against that nasty- looking cloud, you were *also* in the land of nod. Do you sleep a lot?'

Mr Minevar hates interruptions, but I had to guillotine

what would have become a myth-riddled monologue. He gave me his look of disapproval.

Then the pause. Then the quotation.

'"There is a time for many words and then there is also a time for sleep." Homer, laddie, Homer.'

'Have you ever written a poem about sleep, Mr Minevar?'

'Indeed, I have.'

And there was a momentary chest inflation: pride.

'So have I.'

My comment was crisp, curt and sharp; why I don't know. But his left eyebrow raised a little, much in the way of the late Mr Roger Moore: surprise and, one might almost say, amusement in equal measure. But before he could elevate said eyebrow another millimetre I let rip (well, more of a ripple really).

> 'Whenever I want to go to sleep
> Often I count up to one hundred sheep
> And when they're safe within their pen
> If I still awake, I start again.'

I ignored Mr Minevar's snort of derision and continued.

> 'For me sleep-loss is self-destruction
> My mind and body disconnect
> I comb my teeth and brush my ears
> In short, I am completely wrecked—'

'Oh God, stop! Stop! Cease your trivial drivel and twittering.'

And Mr Minevar held his head in his hands: stress. Now you can imagine I was hugely upset by the man's distinct lack of enthusiasm. Of course, the Minevar was oblivious to all this. So now I had to listen to the egomaniac. To say he likes the sound of his own voice is an understatement. Another lesson was to be heard.

'Sleep is not passive; oh no, science has shown that the brain is *active*; metabolically on fire so to speak – removing toxins, safeguarding memory. Now the removal of toxins is done by specialised cells called microglias. Remember that word; microglias. Moreover, they are part of our immune system that reduces inflammation as well as promoting neuronal growth.'

Mr Minevar had a sip of cocktail, before adding: 'I look on them as "nurture cells". With me so far?'

'Yes, Mr Minevar.'

But I was struggling.

'Shakespeare, as ever, was prescient when he wrote it is "sleep that knits up the ravelled sleeve of care". Macbeth, laddie, Macbeth.'

'Yes, I've heard that quotation, Mr Minevar.'

'Indeed, and when one thinks of sleep, one will be reminded of Freud, dreams, nightmares and insomnia.'

There was a dramatic pause, so typical of the man; a deep breath and then the pronouncement, 'I believe it was Thomas Dekker who said "sleep is the golden chain that ties health and bodies together". Anyway, here is my little scribble that touches on *all* of the above.'

And this is what I heard:

> 'Unlocking the unconscious mind
> Was the life work of Sigmund Freud.
> Dreams were in need of interpretation

Though Jung's opinion got Freud annoyed—'

'Oh yes, I remember, Mr Minevar, their friendship faltered.'
'Indeed so, but to continue:

> For Freud the dream was of high importance
> Often a symbol of repressed desire.
> Whilst for Blake it was a God-connection
> Seeing Seraphim, the heavenly choir.
>
> And what of nightmares, ghosts and ghouls?
> There's a classic painting by H. Fuseli
> A sleeping lady lies on her bed
> And an incubus squats upon her belly—'

'Another question, Mr Minevar—'
'Oh heavens, poetical interruptus again! What now? I suppose you want to know about Mr Fuseli.'
'Yes, please. But what is an incubus?'
'It is a male demon intent on having sex with a sleeping lady.'

Well, that answered the question.

'But pray tell me about Mr Fuseli.'
'Fuseli was born in Zurich and died in Putney. I believe he lived from 1741 to 1825. He illustrated works of Shakespeare and Milton and was a master of chiaroscuro. You are familiar with this luscious word, I hope?'

'Well actually, Mr Minevar, no.'

'Oh dear. I thought as much – it is the handling of light and dark for dramatic effect.'

'What was the name of his painting with that incubus

thingy sitting on the lady's tummy?'

'*The Nightmare*; his most famous work. It is both mysterious and erotic and it was a favourite of Freud as it dipped a toe into the unconscious. In fact, Fuseli said, "one of the most unexplored regions of art is the dream."'

'Is there anything else I should know about Mr Fuseli?'

'Goodness, you are becoming a culture vulture. Well, he made a big impression on my hero William Blake, and both Fuseli and Blake had a high regard for Michelangelo. Does that satisfy your thirst for knowledge?'

'You haven't told me his Christian name.'

'Henry. Now if you don't mind, I'll return to my poem:

> The circadian rhythm concerning Man
> Is governed by the degree of light.
> Its silent beat controls the mind;
> We are awake by day, asleep at night.
>
> So how much sleep is good for you?
> Eight hours seems to be the preferred number.
> Science says the range is short,
> Say six to nine for a decent slumber.
>
> MRI scans, EEGs
> Record what's happening within our head.
> Much rewiring, detoxifying
> The brain's so active it must be said—'

'EEGs, Mr Minevar?'

"Electroencephalograms, don't interrupt!'

'Mr Minevar, may I continue with *my* little offering?'

'No!'

But his whole attitude towards me was beginning to grate and, for once, my assertive gene, located on chromosome eight, was ready for action and I was determined to take over the reins. I persisted and much to my delight there was little in the way of remonstrance from Mr M, so I began my poem. Yes, dear reader, *my* poem; lightweight and fluffy, I know, but I just had to do it:

> 'My problem is my excess weight,
> My tummy's fat; so is my rear.
> My collar size exceeds nineteen,
> And so I suffer from sleep apnoea.
>
> And that's the cause of many things;
> Heart attack, stroke, shortness of breath
> Loss of memory and depression.
> Risks if untreated : untimely death.
>
> Which means my sleep is much disturbed
> Unless I use my C-PAP machine,
> Delivering much-needed oxygen
> The normal rate a steady stream.
>
> And then of course there is the dream
> When you can fly at the speed of light,
> Or have the strength of ten thousand men
> And with trolls and dragons and giants fight.
>
> And nightmares are the bane of sleeping
> Often there is a recurring theme;

> Confronted by a horde of zombies,
> Your partner startled by your scream.'

'Have you quite finished?'

'Flinty' would describe the tone of his voice.

'Yes, but don't forget insomnia, Mr Minevar.'

Chromosome eight was still functioning but getting weaker. Satisfied with his afternoon's work, he was about to take a chromosomal siesta.

'Indeed, I will not.'

Well, truth be told, I was pleased to have said my piece. The stage was his once more. He was in his element, and I had escaped being atomised by the Minevar.

'I shall just give you a couple more verses. Note the quotation you are about to hear is from Charlotte Brontë.'

'I know of Charlotte.'

'Good. And so, to finish our unexpected and unwanted duet:

> "A ruffled mind makes a restless pillow"
> As insomniacs know to their cost.
> A mind besieged by woe and worry
> So many hours of sleep are lost.
>
> I'll take my leave with words from Shakespeare
> Whose sagacity runs so true, so deep
> "We are such stuff as dreams are made on
> Our little life (is) rounded with a sleep".

'One is always in debt to the Bard. Every nook and cranny was touched by Shakespeare: life, love, death, the Bard is your man.'

'Gosh, yes, Shakespeare was *so* gifted, wasn't he?'

'Indeed so, a genius. He speaks of "O gentle sleep, Nature's soft nurse".'

Mr Minevar emitted a soft cough.

'Yes, a good night's sleep leaves one feeling refreshed.'

I could see where this was heading and I was right.

'Talking of being refreshed, I wonder if I could tap you for another tipple; A <u>Manhattan</u>†† perhaps. Manhattan, a densely populated area of New York; the city that never sleeps.'

'An excellent choice, Mr Minevar. Oh, look at my wallet; it's losing weight.'

Well, a wee bit of sarcasm could do no harm.

'No worries, Mr Minevar. I'll just make my way to the bar again.'

And, looking back at him, there was a distinct kind of grin on his face. One could say he almost looked a little sheepish.

---

†† Whisky, sweet vermouth and bitters.

THE WAR OF THE POESIES

The next section was not on Mr Minevar's list, for a very good reason that will soon become apparent. What you are about to read is a deadly duel of words: <u>The War of the Poesies</u>. Of course, there have been spats between literary figures – one thinks of Mr Gore Vidal and Mr Norman Mailer. But some of that, to my mind, involved a bit of shadow boxing. Mr Minevar meant business; the sword was unsheathed, the gun loaded, the grenade unpinned. It just needed a catalyst, the magazine, *Poets of Today*.

Now, Mr Minevar can be a sensitive soul. A man of complexity, sometimes affable, occasionally indifferent but often, yes oh so often, irascible; especially when the critics have, with sharp talons, torn holes in his poetic cloth. His worst enemy in this respect is, without a doubt, Dr Richard Arbuthnot. I have alluded to him in an earlier poem. Holmes had Moriarty, Bond had Blofeld and Mr Minevar's nemesis is this bastard Arbuthnot. I have met him and he is the worst kind of reptile. I once asked Mr Minevar where he lived. Acknowledging his ill-earned wealth, Mr Minevar replied, 'In his Palace of Lies, in Hades.'

So, let us return to the peaceful setting of the beer garden of the George and Dragon; quite apt if you were to view Arbuthnot as the dragon. We were sipping our cocktails: <u>Manhattans</u>, you will remember. Alf had returned to form; they were delicious. Mr Minevar started the conversation:

'What's in your briefcase?'

'Nothing, Mr Minevar.'

' "Nothing will become of nothing"; Lear, laddie. But why do you carry nothing with you?' And before I could say anything, he had conjured out of the briefcase the magazine *Poets of Today* that has both built and destroyed the lives of so many poets. Leaving the other contents (plain paper and pens) within the briefcase, Mr Minevar started to read his review by Dr Richard Arbuthnot. Oh dear, it breaks my heart to relate the incident and it was with an excess of apprehension, moist eyes and even moister armpits that I heard the following:

'Minevar is an abomination to the written word. He makes no attempt at craftsmanship. His poems are vacuous, just like the man; all fluff and guff. Some critics, borrowing a phrase from the illustrious American William Penn, say Minevar's poems have "more sail than ballast", but to my mind they have neither sail nor ballast. His ship is in the doldrums. He is a nothing man going nowhere.'

'Can I have my magazine back please, Mr Minevar?'

'No.'

He read on:

<u>'In Praise of Mr Minevar. By Dr Richard Arbuthnot</u>
If brevity is the soul of wit
Minevar's works are the opposite.

> His longer poems alter Time
> As they never ever seem to end.
> He struggles hard to find a rhyme
> Which drives the reader round the bend.
>
> He plods his way to God knows where
> And stretches syntax that breaks Hooke's Law.
> No iambic bounce to lead you on;
> In short, his writing's extremely poor.
>
> You're reading guff that has no weight
> So long and tedious, so very dreary.
> No end in sight with sinking heart
> You're left bereft and feeling weary.
>
> Tired and confused and at wit's end
> One yawn a minute's the going rate.
> But if the poem exceeds half an hour
> Your yawning will accelerate.
>
> There is no poet worse than him
> Take my advice; put down his work.
> No poetic muse has touched his brain
> The man's a witless twit, a berk.'

'Bit mean that, Mr Minevar.'

Mr Minevar's face was red. Farrow and Ball would have named it 'Ferocious Red'.

'Mean? Did you say *mean*? The man is a snake, a cobra, but I shall mongoose him yet.'

I watched Mr Minevar with growing fascination. He was undergoing further colour changes like a dyspeptic cuttlefish which has overindulged its crab lunch.

'Oh, how he mocks me, the scurrilous scoundrel! I am a fish, filleted and fried. No, no, it is *he* who is the fish. COD: C͟hurlish O͟bnoxious D͟espicable. But I shall reel him in yet.'

'So, you think he's eel-vil", eh, Mr Minevar?' I said, trying a dash of humour to keep afloat the fishy comments. But Mr Minevar was in no mood for piscine jokes; the beast within him was awake.

'Here, take this tissue of bilge and read to me.'

'Well, there's not much more.'

'There is, there is. Is this a chalice of poison I see before me?'

'No, it's your cocktail. Mr Minevar, you are not well.'

'Read on, boy, I am aroused. I am flayed and I have fever. Oh heavens, he has unzipped my spine, the swine! Read on, make haste.'

And so, I read Dr Arbuthnot's second contribution to the *Poets of Today* magazine.

'Mr Minevar by Dr Richard Arbuthnot
Overrated, overpraised,
His work mere fluff; you get nothing from it.
Except it makes you tired and nauseous
So reach for a bowl, retch then vomit.'

'Zounds!' exclaimed Mr Minevar, resorting to an eighteenth-century expletive. 'Lord, how I do detest the man. The libellous lizard. Read on, laddie. I am of a sweat but read on.'

> 'He writes just like a worn-out hack
> You search in vain to find humour.
> To keep awake, you must caffeinate
> And wish the poem would end sooner'

'Beelzebub! Odious worm! Read on! Read on!'

> 'His poems render you exhausted
> With eyelids drooping its true to say
> You've nearly lost the will to live.
> A coma just one page away.'

'Oh, the dog! Oh, the warty toad! Oh, how my heart jumps! Oh, my palpitations! But no, no, I'll *not* be unhinged by his vile verse. Read on, I'm losing focus, you're blurred, laddie. Have my eyeballs shrunk in their sockets?'

'No, Mr Minevar, in fact there is a bit of a bulge, right worse than the left.'

'You're fuzzy. I am weak at the knees, but I shall not fall. Read on!'

'You're not well, George.'

'Read on!'

> 'With supreme effort the last page is turned
> It's hard to explain just how you feel.
> You pray to God he won't write another;
> You've survived, thank God, the ordeal.'

'Are not his words a dagger to my heart? This man has bile for blood. But I will serve a dish that is *not* cold. No, Mr Shakespeare, my dish will be hot. He will combust!

The brazen bounder has gone too far. In Zeus's name I shall unleash a thunderbolt. Yes, a thunderbolt. Have you a pen?'

'Yes, Mr Minevar.'

'Paper, I must have paper!'

'Just a minute.'

'No, paper *now* before the muse disappears. Ah woe! She is going and I am left with her shadow. No matter. Dr Arbuthnot shall feel the heat from my pen, I promise.'

And it is true to say that Mr Minevar kept to his feeling and promise.

'Strap yourself in, laddie. It's going to be a bumpy ride.

<u>Homage to Dr Richard Arbuthnot. The Bastard.</u>
Now hear this, Dr Arbuthnot
You think you're master of the pen,
But I've read your works, Dr Arbuthnot
And perhaps it's time to think again

Because your prose is so anaemic
Your poetry so short of wit
Verbs suffocate amongst the verbiage.
Get thee gone to your snake-pit

And join the other viper-critics
Yes, that's the place where you belong.
You vile and legless loathsome creature
Of mirthless lips and forked tongue

I've heard you hiss and spit your venom.
You think you're funny and rather clever.

In fact, you're dull and oh-so boring
Your brain much lighter than a feather.

Your work stagnates through lack of learning,
With one lone neuron you criticise.
Not comprehending what you're reading
So from other critics you plagiarise.

You believe half-rhyming is your forte;
I hope my poem has not been too harsh
But as far as I'm concerned, Arbuthnot,
You can stick your reviews right up your arse.'

'Chew on that, Arbuthnot,' said Mr Minevar.

'Bit crude, Mr M – the ending I mean. But a veritable bullseye. Crikey, you *really* don't like him, do you?'

'No, I do not. He's a balloon that needs pricking. He's toxic; the Cane Toad of literary criticism. Oh no! More paper. The muse beckons me. The pen; paper. Yes, yes, I warm again to the challenge. Oh my God, can no one douse the fire in my brain? Arbuthnot, you shall rue the day you crossed swords with the Minevar. Listen….listen, can you not hear Mistress Muse a-whispering?'

'No, George, I cannot. I think you are not well.'

And, believe me, it is no exaggeration to say that his eyes flashed, his face twitched and his tongue flicked in and out like the tongue of a Komodo dragon as his pen scratched out a new work, with only one target in the crosswires: Dr Arbuthnot.

'<u>Introducing Dr Arbuthnot to the Human Race.</u>
So, Dr Arbuthnot, you fucked-up fiend,

Why so hostile to poor old me?
Although your efforts are so puny
Please accept my wrath and enmity.

Oh dear Arbuthnot, my dear Arbuthnot
I do not want to duel with you
But send by post this poetic letter
As no phone, email or text will do.

Oh dear Arbuthnot, my dear Arbuthnot
Please climb down from your high horse.
In manners you are *so* uncouth;
Your writing's worse; the text so coarse.

I know you were not of woman born
But reptile like Blake's *Ghost of a Flea*.
Evil spells made you that monster
Formed from slime beneath the sea.

And I wonder how you got your job
Becoming a so-called reviewer.
They say you're brash and rather snobbish
Said by many, no words are truer.

So, Arbuthnot, put down your pen
And change to something that's worthwhile.
Botox to smooth away your wrinkles;
Erase that frown, please learn to smile,

And you will find that *when* you smile
The world becomes a better place

> And I shall take you by your claw
> And let you meet the human race.'

'Dodge that one, you slimeball. Hah! You have been torpedoed.'

With some relief, I was aware that Mr Minevar's speech was becoming ever so slightly less stratospheric. 'Two things, Mr Minevar. One, your colour has almost returned to normal, but two, you look a bit dry, as if you have been kiln-baked. All your well-earned sweat seems to have evaporated with the heat of your passion. So, what's your poison, Mr M?'

'I rather fancy a rum and coke, laddie. Not too much coke, mind.'

'Don't go away. I'll be back in a jiffy.'

'You're very kind.'

In fact, I was back in *half* a jiffy and the glass of rum and coke was full to the brim (50% rum, 50% coke). And there was just a hint of a smile on his face. A bit like the *Mona Lisa*; just a smidgen.

THE CONFESSIONS OF TOBY WELLS

'This is paradise, is it not, Mr Minevar?'

'Why do you say that?'

'Well, here we are in the beer garden; surrounded by trees, the heavy scent of honeysuckle, bees and butterflies seeking out nectar, and we are drinking our *own* sort of nectar; rum and coke in the warm sunshine. It's so peaceful, almost spiritual.'

'You do make it sound like the Garden of Eden.'

As usual there was a pause. It was my turn to blow on the embers; ignite the conversation. So I did.

'Do you believe in original sin, Mr Minevar?'

Mr Minevar thought for a moment, then spoke.

'No, I do not. If my brain is functioning, I believe it relates to the fall of Adam and Eve- when they ate the apple in the Garden of Eden. Yes, by this action they lumbered Mankind with guilt and sin from birth. Nonsense. But that is why early baptism is deemed by many to be so important.'

Another pause.

'No, a sinful life is much more complicated than that.'

'Yes, Mr Minevar. I think you are right.'

'I am.'

Just following this immodest remark, I noticed a couple of butterflies engaged in aerial courtship. Then, a thought popped into my head.

'Mr Minevar – oh, I must remember to call you George – it's odd how we attach importance to certain numbers. I mean three is important for religious reasons: the Holy Trinity, three crosses on Calvary, three days before His resurrection.'

'Three Wise Men,' added Mr Minevar, who seemed to be showing some sort of interest in my ramblings.

'Then there is "Faith, Hope and Charity". *The Three Musketeers*. The kindergarten song *"Three Blind Mice"*.' I could feel my brain doing a few press ups.

'And Mr Minevar, just think of all those countries whose flags are a combination of three colours: Great Britain, France, Belgium, Holland, America. Oh, and the song, *"Three Coins in a Fountain"*.'

I gave the old noodle a bit more exercise: 3+4=7.

'Now, number seven is also significant, George. In ancient Egypt, it symbolised eternal life.'

'Indeed so.'

'Then there is *Snow White and the Seven Dwarves* and that great film *The Magnificent Seven*.'

'Indeed so.'

I could feel my brain throbbing as a result of this workout.

'Also, George, there are *The Seven Wonders Of The Ancient World* like *The Great Pyramid of Giza* and *The Hanging Gardens of Babylon*.'

'Indeed so.'

'Oh yes,' I said, still ploughing my furrow. 'There are also *Seven Wonders* of more recent times like *The Taj Mahal, Machu Picchu* and *The Great Wall of China* to name but three.'

Mr Minevar made no attempt to stifle a yawn. It was his way of communicating that he was beginning to get restless and bored. I took a sip from my rum and coke.

'Oh, there is also a drink called *7Up*.'

'Laddie, I am drowning in numbers; send me a lifeline. Something meaty, something a poet can get his teeth into. And don't say there are seven days in a week.'

'Well, Earth has seven seas'

'Try again'

'I'm rather fond of the Sussex coast, I've a soft spot for the *Seven Sisters*.'

'Try again.'

'What about Rome? It is such a beautiful city .It has seven hills you know'

'Try again'

'Oh, wait a minute, George, what about the *Seven Deadly Sins*?'

'At last! At last, we have arrived at our destination. That was a very long gestation.'

'I apologise, George, I didn't realise we were on a journey. With regards to sins, wasn't it Shakespeare who wrote, "the tempter or the tempted, who sins most?" What do you think, George?'

'That is indeed a question for contemplation, but alas time is short and the poem is long.'

'Not *too* long, I hope, Mr Minevar?'

For some reason, 'George' had been usurped by 'Mr

Minevar' again.

'And I shall tell you why, Mr Minevar. I tried to read *Paradise Lost* and I'm afraid I ran out of steam. Then I read that Dr Johnson commented on the epic poem, saying "none wished it longer".'

'Indeed, that is so. Now without further ado I shall proceed.'

'Has it a title, Mr Minevar?'

An innocent question which annoyed my master.

'Heavens, have your microglias cells ceased to function? Yes, yes it has a title. Now listen with both ears. Ears open, mouth shut.

<u>The Confessions of Mr Toby Wells.</u>

<u>Toby</u>: 'Oh help me Father for I have sinned
And my dearest wish is to go to heaven.
To so many vices I have succumbed
Not one or two, they number seven.

Pernicious <u>pride</u> and evil <u>envy</u>
<u>Gluttony</u>, <u>lust</u>, <u>greed</u>, and <u>sloth</u>
Have ripped apart my whole being
And left me angry, filled with <u>wrath.</u>

<u>Father Flynn</u>: All right, my son, I am all ears
Let's take each vice, one by one.
Be rest assured, all will be well
You'll be forgiven when we are done.

<u>Toby</u>: Oh Father Flynn, I'm full of pride
As I've just got the best degree,
Beating all my fellow students,

Who studied Art and History.

<u>Father Flynn</u>: Toby, pride leads to arrogance
The remedy is so plain to see.
Take heed of what Christ has to say
And take on board <u>humility</u>.

<u>Toby</u>: Oh Father Flynn, I'm full of envy
My house is small; my neighbour's big
And I want his enormous garden
With a veggie plot in which to dig.

<u>Father Flynn</u>: Toby, envy is an intense emotion
For something that you really crave
But <u>kindness</u> cures this evil sin
By teaching how one should behave.

<u>Toby</u>: Oh Father Flynn, I am a glutton
My penchant is for Christmas cake
But also doughnuts, sweets galore
Eggs and chips and sirloin steak.'

'I like steak and chips, Mr Minevar.'
But he put his finger to his lips to silence me. Quite civil really. Anyway, he continued on the sin of gluttony.

'Toast and jam, honeyed ham.
Vol-au-vents and beef stew
Bakewell tart, bread and cheese
Tea and coffee and my homebrew.'
'Crikey, Mr Minevar, it makes you peckish hearing all the

food and drink.'

Another finger, but this one was not pressed to his lips; it was jerked upwards. Not so civil.

> Father Flynn: Toby, the solution is so very simple
> Self-control will make the difference;
> Better for your health and wallet,
> Adhere to a new <u>temperance</u>.

> Toby: Oh Father Flynn, I am filled with lust
> For my neighbour, Mrs Wright,
> Aged forty, curvaceous, oozing sex,
> I lust for her both day and night.

> Father Flynn: Now Toby, lust is hormone-driven
> A fact of science, you may depend
> To cool the blood, damp down your loins
> You must make <u>chastity</u> your friend.

> Toby: Oh Father Flynn, I am so greedy
> Ever wanting more and more.
> My wallet closed, they call me Scrooge
> And I look down upon the poor.'

'Whoa, Mr Minevar, may I intrude?'

'Another premature ejaculation. What have you to say this time?'

'Well, it is a quote from Darwin. He said, "If the misery of the poor be caused not by laws of nature but by our institutions, great is our sin."'

'Yes, indeed. Charles was a kind man, empathetic, though

it has to be said he was somewhat cocooned in his large house in Kent. A shy man but quite unlike many Victorians in that he was a wonderful family man; not strict at all. But to continue with Father Flynn, who has been most patient while we have become a teeny-bit tangential.

> Father Flynn: Toby, excess truly rots the soul
> You've named it well, 'tis called greed.
> The antidote needs no doctor's note;
> It's <u>charity</u> that you need.

> Toby: Oh Father Flynn, I am so lazy
> I want to spend all day in bed.
> It's just that I can't be bothered
> And I'm work-shy, it must be said.

> Father Flynn: Toby, if laziness has taken hold
> And work lost all of its appeal,
> Roll up your sleeves; change your ways,
> Enjoy the things you do with <u>zeal</u>.

> Toby: Oh Father Flynn, I'm wracked by wrath
> 'Cos all these sins have ruined me
> And gouged out all that once was good
> Now Hell will be my destiny.

> Father Flynn: Toby, wrath is anger multiplied
> To soothe the soul, pray each day
> Be <u>patient</u> and then you will find
> That wrath quite fast will go away.

'Mr Minevar, may I interrupt?'

'If you must.'
'Well it's from Blake; I'm sure you know it:

> I was angry with my friend
> I told my wrath, the wrath did end
> I was angry with my foe
> I told it not, the wrath did grow.'

'Ah, dear wise William. From his poem '*A Poison Tree*'; would that he were alive today. But to continue:

> <u>Toby</u>: Oh, thank you, Father, for what you've said
> Your words of wisdom have eased my pain
> But alas, dear Father within a month,
> I'll need to relate my sins again.

> <u>Father Flynn</u>: Toby, you can of course return to me
> But heed my words, give them some thought
> And you will find within a week
> Your seven sins reduced to nought.

'Bravo Father Flynn!' I cried out. 'A very pleasant man, Mr Minevar.'
'Yes, and I should add, extremely patient.'
'Mr Minevar, do you think Toby will return?'
'Oh yes, undoubtedly. If I were to rewrite the poem, I would have probably called him Arnold. He'll be back.'
'Gosh, Mr Minevar, that really was a long poem; I expect you have worked up a bit of a thirst.'
'Indeed, I have. A <u>Pina Colada</u>,‡‡ if you please.'

---

‡‡ Pineapple, rum, and coconut cream.

'Very PC!' I quipped. 'To say is to do, George; back in a flash.'

On returning, I was greeted by an enormous grin of Cheshire Cat proportion. Then, just like the grin of the Cat, it slowly disappeared.

'It's funny,' said Mr Minevar, 'what stimulus can stir up memories. For Proust it was the Madeline; for many it is music or a particular perfume; for me it is alcohol.'

'Is there anything you wish to share with me, Mr Minevar?'

Mr Minevar looked hard into my face and then said quietly, almost as if speaking to himself.

'No, I'd rather not. No, I'd rather not.'

And I felt it best to cease questioning and wondered whether my Pina Colada would conjure up any memories. It didn't.

LITTLE OWL

'Well now, Mr Minevar, you're not drinking your Pina Colada. It's delicious. The barman, Alf, asked me whether I wanted a couple of little umbrellas but I declined.'

There was no 'cocktail comment', instead Mr Minevar looked sad and said, 'I fear we are nearly at the end of our journey. But, as you know, I have one more offering.'

'Oh good, so, Mr Minevar, what is your last poem about – animal, vegetable or mineral? I'm afraid I've forgotten.'

'Animal.'

'Not another insect, Mr Minevar?'

'No. I'm upset you've forgotten. For my last poem we take to the air.'

'Bat, bird or butterfly' I thought, but before I could deliver my thoughts Mr Minevar proclaimed, 'Owl, remember? In particular the Little Owl (*Athene noctua*).'

'Well, we are ascending the tree of life at any rate, Mr Minevar, but why this particular creature?'

'Many reasons. They have a fascinating relationship with humans. In Ancient Greece, they epitomised wisdom and prudence.'

'Why the association with wisdom, Mr Minevar? After all, they *are* bird-brained?'

'Indeed so, but the Little Owl was one of the symbols adopted by Athena. It was said that the owl, which can rotate its head either way two hundred and seventy degrees, could see into areas that were not apparent to Athena and that enabled her to see Truth.

'Winnie the Pooh often sought advice from Owl, Mr Minevar,' and I had a feeling I had taken the conversation down a notch or two.

'Indeed, that is so.'

'My theory, Mr Minevar, is that they have a kind of human face and there is something about their eyes which speaks of sagacity.'

'For once you have shown perception. I agree with you. The eyes have it.'

'But not the nose,' I quipped, alerting Mr Minevar to the fact that I was aware of our parliamentary voting system.

'There is no nose, laddie; just nostrils at the base of the beak.'

So, no sense of humour, compliment with condescension; never untainted praise.

'Well, Mr Minevar, I await your verse.' Irritated by his attitude, there was a slight edge to my voice, but it cut no ice with Mr M.

'Wait no longer, I have just heard the starting gun.' And off he went.

<u>'Little Owl</u>
I'm watching you, Mr Owl
Perched up high on cedar tree

And wonder what it is you're thinking
Whilst you stare, unblinking, watching me.

To me you seem so statuesque,
So still and solid and somehow wise.
I think your wisdom needs explanation;
It lies within those staring eyes.

Those eyes which give binocular vision
Aiding you to capture prey,
Sucking in the fading light
That signifies the end of day.

'Actually, Mr Minevar, the Little Owl does its hunting in daylight—'
'Yes, I know, you potato. I am merely commenting on the Little Owl's excellent vision,' said a slightly irritated Mr Minevar.

'And all around birds are roosting
Moths and bats have taken flight.
But still you stare with eyes unblinking
As you and I both enter night.'

'Gosh, Mr Minevar, I can sense a connection between you and the owl.'
"Indeed so. But to continue:

It's true while other birds chat and twitter
You stay silent and speak no word.
Whilst other birds move around quite frantic
You sit and stare; oh unruffled bird.

> And Athens took you to her bosom
> And stamped your image so all could see
> On silver coins that spoke of riches
> Power, Wisdom : Democracy.'

'I'm with you there, Mr Minevar. Animals have played a large part in human history. Not just food, drink, travel, and clothes, but also warfare. Horses, for instance, and then there is Hannibal with his elephants and of course—'

'Quite so. Shall I continue with my poem?'

Then he added, 'I would that you were a swan.'

'Why so, Mr Minevar?'

'Mute.'

But I was becoming like one of Hannibal's elephants, thick-skinned and virtually impervious to his barbed comments. When I made no comment, he continued:

> 'I'm watching you, Mr Owl
> Fly off from high on cedar tree
> What *was* the thought that set you flying
> Into the darkness leaving me?'

'Oh, Mr Minevar, that is a wee bit ambiguous. Were you being deserted by the owl or were you radiating a kind of darkness?'

'Quite so. A veritable bullseye would be your expression. You must choose, but think before you speak.'

Well, the cocktails had taken their toll and I could not choose. Instead, I became somewhat whimsical and came to the conclusion that if my thoughts were to have colour, they would be sepia. For some reason, I felt a sense of loss mingled with nostalgia – was it because this might be the last time I would see Mr Minevar or was it because the dreams of my youth had not come to fruition? Maybe both, maybe one, maybe neither. All I know is the colour in my mind's eye was sepia. And Mr Minevar would have taken great delight in telling me it was the brown pigment obtained from the common cuttlefish: '*Sepia officinalis*, surely you know that?' Oh, you are a cocky sod, Mr Minevar. Cocky, rude, condescending, irascible, conceited, but so much part of my life. No, Mr Minevar, I want you to live forever. More than anything I have wished for, you must not die. Be immortal like your bloody Greek gods. 'Sepia, laddie, used by Leonardo da Vinci, you may have heard the name.' Yes, that's what he might have said.

I stared at Mr Minevar who was looking skywards with a head rotation well short of the two hundred and seventy degrees of our Little Owl. I soon found out what had caught his attention.

'If I am not mistaken, there is a Pipistrelle bat flitting around the beer garden, and I too must take flight. I fear I must owe you something for the drinks. Have you taken note of what has been imbibed?'

'Indeed, I have, Mr Minevar; quite a list as it happens. I have included the name of the spirit relevant to each drink:

1.	French Connection	Cognac.
2.	Singapore Sling	Gin. Cherry brandy.
3.	XYZ	Rum.
4.	Lion's Tail	Bourbon
5.	Red Snapper	Gin.
6.	Hurricane	Light rum. Dark rum.

7.	Manhattan	Whisky.
8.	Rum & Coke	Rum.
9.	Pina Colada	Rum.

'Extremely Epicurean, is it not, Mr Minevar? But it is my treat, Mr Minevar, I mean, George.'

'Thank goodness!' said Mr Minevar. 'For I have no money. I was banking on your largesse. I thank thee.'

'Well thank you, George, for your time.'

I made no comment about short arms and deep pockets. I continued to speak.

'I hope we can meet again soon.'

But there was no answer. Instead, he shook me by the hand, and with slow lumbering movements, he entered the twilight, zigzagging his way homewards to leave me with my thoughts. I found myself whispering to myself, 'I wish you health and happiness, Mr Minevar, I really do, and may you have better fortune.' No sooner had I spoken these words, I heard the hooting of an owl. And I heard myself saying out loud, 'Probably a Tawny Owl, Mr Minevar, certainly not your Little Owl.' And I too tottered home, clutching my house keys and empty wallet. Post-Minevar, always an empty wallet.

EPILOGUE

It would not have escaped your notice that the quantity of alcohol imbibed by Mr Minevar was matched by my good self. Not surprisingly, the following day found me somewhat worse for wear. On rummaging through my bedside drawer, seeking out medication, I found a crumpled piece of paper which had yellowed slightly, in keeping with its age. For the sake of Minevarian completeness, I have included it as one of his works.

<u>My Hero</u>
My hero is the poet William McGonagall
Without his influence I would not write anything at all.
I read and read his poems with admiration
His verse is truly a gift to our Nation.
Sometimes the sentences can be very very long when the
Spirit of the poetic muse, for a long time, he has caught.
Other times they're short.

And though his poem '*The Tay Bridge Disaster*'
Rhymes badly: in other poems he could finally master
The knack of rhyming without them sounding too odd,

Though at times they still did for which I must thank God.
As that was what people found so amusing.
Rest assured there was no chance of him losing
His gift of bad verse;
McGonagall my hero, the poet, none worse.

George Edward Minevar, aged 15.

Did the young Minevar really think McGonagall was so mind-numbingly bad that he was good, or did the young poet have his adolescent tongue planted firmly in his cheek? Only George Edward Minevar can answer that question.

THE POPE AND THE PECKERHEAD

There is one other poem I have included as a means of showing how Mr Minevar's poetry has matured since his teenage offering. This latter poem was an early broadside fired by Mr Minevar against that most unpleasant man, Dr Richard Arbuthnot. Mr Minevar was in his mid-thirties, responding to a most virulent attack on his poetic style. I feel that Mr Minevar was quite restrained in his response. It is called '<u>The Pope and the Peckerhead</u>' and contrasts the style of Alexander Pope with the vacuous prose of Dr Arbuthnot. 'Peckerhead' I believe means 'idiot', and this is what he had written:

> If brevity is the soul of wit,
> Longevity is just the opposite,
> I.e., witty folks like Pope and Shaw
> Do inform us, 'less is more'.

> Praise <u>God</u> for Alexander Pope!
> Verse deadlier than the hangman's rope.

Sulphuric venom stemmed from his pen,
Burned egos of so many men.

So small of frame, so big of brain
His pithy words could cause such pain.
So cutting were his words in verse
That diced Pomposity and worse.

Surgeon-precise, denouncing vice,
Words born of fire; cold as ice.
A sniper's touch 'tis true had he
Gone one by one the Enemy.

With irony, epigrams galore
A literary magician to the fore.
Word-tricks abound in good measure
That polish aphoristic treasure.

Pure gold, the Midas Touch had he
Diminishing Man's vanity,
Skewering any verse 'twas bad
Consider his work, the '*Dunciad*'.

Here, Laureate Cibber becomes at once,
A foolish man, a fucked-up dunce;
His work shown full of empty space
Befitting such a basket-case.

Then compare Pope with the plumbic prose
Of Arbuthnot – God only knows
Although he writes both day and night
He never seems to get it right.

2 Alexander Pope (1688–1744)

Writing stuff of *no* import
With little brain, *no* trace of thought.
So limited in his scope
Compared with our sagacious Pope.

Mundane, so boring man and prose
And, as everybody knows
His lengthy works so bereft of wit
So suit a man who's such a sh*t.

Imagine Arbuthnot were a lord
With ermined gown and belted sword;
No sword for Pope; no just his pen
Emasculating such-like men.

So, let's rejoice, give praise to Pope!
Whose acerbic wit gives us hope
That we can say with one accord
The Pen is mightier than the Sword.

It was Voltaire who said, 'To hold a pen is to be at war'. Well, as you are aware, the battle between these two adversaries is still ongoing. Only time will tell who prevails.

ACKNOWLEDGEMENTS

I should like to thank Troubador for all their help with the production of this book. Their support and guidance were invaluable.

Special thanks must be given to Beth Archer, Production Controller. Patience is a virtue and she has it in spades.

Lastly but certainly not least, my heart felt thanks to my children, Will and Imo. Will typed and amended the manuscript and Imo painted the pictures of Mr Minevar, Henry VIII and Alexander Pope.

This book is printed on paper from sustainable sources managed under the Forest Stewardship Council (FSC) scheme.

It has been printed in the UK to reduce transportation miles and their impact upon the environment.

For every new title that Matador publishes, we plant a tree to offset CO_2, partnering with the More Trees scheme.

MORE TREES
LET'S PLANT A BILLION TREES

For more about how Matador offsets its environmental impact, see www.troubador.co.uk/about/